STRESS
FIRST AID

FOR THE WORKING
WOMAN

HOW TO KEEP COOL
WHEN YOU'RE UNDER FIRE

Dr. B. J. Epstein

Library of Congress Catalog Card Number 90-86100

ISBN No. 0-9616204-1-2

BECOMING PRESS
P.O. Box 221383
Carmel, CA 93922

ACKNOWLEDGEMENT

I send acknowledgements, loving thoughts, and gratitude to all the people in my life who have caused me the stress I have learned to cope with so well.

CONTENTS

INTRODUCTION

To the stereotype of the overworked stressed male executive has been added the reality of the overstressed woman in the workforce. It is estimated that 90% of all women will be employed outside the home for money at some point in their lives. Traditionally women are childbearers and the primary caretakers of the home and family. This is a full time job. Add a job outside the home and you have two full time jobs. Recent studies show that the average married woman with a family who works outside the home for money, and then plays her traditional homemaker role after work, puts in 85 work hours a week. Multiple roles and overwork are just two of the ingredients of a stressful lifestyle. (Go to PART 4, page 70, of this book and take the STRESS TEST to assess your personal stress level.)

A low-stressful lifestyle is a worthwhile goal. Many people feel they function better and produce more under pressure or stress. I disagree. *Excess* stress brings with it negative emotions and behaviors, low vitality and decreased life satisfaction. Excess stress also results in constant fatigue and a myriad of other physical symptoms. Ultimately, excess stress substantially decreases one's ability to perform to potential. Does the following scenario sound familiar?

Work is piling up, and time pressures are getting you down. Office politics keep you on guard and you don't know where you stand. You have responsibilities, but no real authority to take action. On top of everything else, your company is installing a new computer system and restructuring. You could probably deal with the office stressors if you had some revitalizing time at home, but you can't relax because you have to pick up your toddler at the day care center on the way home. Should you stop at the grocery store first and risk being late to pick up your child, or should you pick him up first and have to deal with a tired, cranky toddler in the crowded grocery store? Oh well, you can make that decision when you find out how late it will be when you finally get out of the office.

When you get home, your excited five-year-old asks you to make a costume for the kindergarten play. You discover that the play is next Friday at 10 a.m., and now you have to choose between two more stressors, taking time off at 10 on Friday or disappointing your child. You put off that decision for now and suggest that Tommy color at the kitchen table until dinner is ready.

At this point, you want to ask your husband to help with dinner, but he looks like he has had a rough day, too, and he is so comfortable with his wine and the newspaper. You think Bill would resent being asked to get up and help you. You might as well do it all yourself. After all, your mother brought you up to be a good wife and mother. She always had a hot, nutritious dinner prepared when your father came home from work. O.K.-- to the sink! As you peel the carrots, the familiar depression hits you again, and you realize that somehow, in the past few years, you have gotten lost. You haven't taken time to do anything for yourself and the bright, optimistic, energetic person you were has disappeared.

You work in a tense atmosphere all day, fight the traffic after work, and then care for noisy children and a tired husband in the evenings. The weekends are taken up with the administrative details of living. Your life seems to be controlled by circumstances and by other people. You wonder about the choices you have made and think it is too late to do anything about them. You love your family, and your income is necessary to live the lifestyle you and your husband have chosen. Your mother warned you about full time work, but you wanted a career and a family. Six years ago you were confident you could handle it all. Now you are not so sure. You feel you have to prove yourself by keeping it all going and doing a good job with everything. After all, your husband does deserve a good wife, and your children deserve a good mother.

Lately, the headaches have increased and you find yourself irritable much of the time. You are so tired after work that you don't fully enjoy your family, and as a matter of fact, they don't enjoy you much either. Your fatigue and distraction take the fun out of being with you. Even sex has lost its appeal.

Work is bringing less and less personal satisfaction, and your productivity continues to suffer. You have noticed yourself taking more trips to the coffee pot and craving more chocolate as a special treat to make you "feel better." You have even had several anxiety attacks in the past few weeks.

*****

I have just described a woman in the early stages of "burnout." She needs immediate coping strategies. If you recognize parts of yourself here, or if you scored high when you took the STRESS TEST in PART 4, you need help to feel better right now. You need FIRST AID. First aid gives immediate short term relief from pain. When you begin to feel some relief, steps then can be taken to deal with the causes of distress, and finally preventive measures can be taken.

This is your STRESS FIRST AID HANDBOOK. It is quick to read, and full of ideas that you can use to alleviate stressors as they present themselves in your life. It is simple and action oriented. This book provides very little information on what stress is, what causes it, and what it actually does to your mind and body, because there are many fine books on stress that cover the topic in great depth. If you are interested in finding out more about stress research or in perfecting other stress reduction techniques, read some of the books on the reading list at the back of this book. For first aid, however, keep *STRESS FIRST AID FOR THE WORKING WOMAN* within reach. You'll then be able to keep cool when you are under fire.

HOW TO USE THIS BOOK

B.J. Epstein's First Law states: *WHEN ALL ELSE FAILS, DO SOMETHING.* I like the action oriented approach that asserts--when you are stressed, determine why, and then do something to fix the problem. In this short simple book I make suggestions for some things you can do. The suggestions work. However, following through is not always easy. I recognize this. Many of the ideas require specific skill. It is not my purpose to give you all the skills you need to live a high productivity, low stress lifestyle. My purpose is to make workable suggestions, and then give you references you can go to if you need more help.

To begin, read PART 1, FIRST AID TIPS FOR STRESSFUL TIMES. Try those ideas that appeal to you. Write down your favorite tips in your ACTION PROGRAM in PART 4. Use these techniques often. When you have learned several ways to make yourself more comfortable, you are ready for the next step.

PART 2 gives you specific ideas for dealing with the everyday stressors that are common in the working woman's experience. After reading these ideas, go to PART 4. There you will write down ideas for dealing with the specific situations that are most stressful for *you*. Perfecting these techniques involves planning and requires practice. But soon you will have a plan for coping rather than reacting in ways that create more stress, further depleting your productive energy. It is far better to feel energized.

You can learn long term strategies for healthful low stress living. These strategies will give you the positive energy you need to function productively. Make the effective stress management strategies in PART 3 an integral part of your life. The new productive lifestyle you can create will prevent many stressors, and give you the physical and emotional strength to cope effectively with the stressors that are not preventable.

In PART 4 you will continue to design your own stress reduction program and expand your useful repertoire of stress control techniques. You will outline the attitude adjustments you can easily make and adopt a lifestyle that will result in long term stress prevention and a healthy, productive, satisfying life. When it is complete, your ACTION PROGRAM will be your personalized quick reference to the stress control techniques that work for you.

PART 1

FIRST AID FOR STRESSFUL TIMES

When you need a quick stress reliever, try these ideas:

- Make a list of the good things in your life.
- Laugh.
- Read something inspirational.
- Listen to a motivational or inspirational audio cassette tape.
- Listen to beautiful music. I find Beethoven and Rachmaninoff especially uplifting. Choose your own favorites.
- Go to a chapel or somewhere quiet to sit and pray or meditate. (Actually you can pray anywhere and any time. It works.)
- Buy yourself a gift or reward. This should be an inexpensive luxury item that you don't really need. Fancy scented soaps or hand creams are good choices. (Stay away from a box of candy.)
- Pamper yourself at a beauty salon. Have your hair done, a facial, manicure, or whatever you enjoy.
- Have a professional massage.
- Run a hot bubble bath, take a book and a cup of tea into the bathroom. Soak. Dry yourself with a large fluffy towel. Smooth a good lotion on your body. If you don't have a luxurious towel and a good body lotion, buy them. (These are good rewards.)
- Go to a movie, concert or play.
- Read fiction or something else that has nothing to do with your work.

- Take a few deep relaxing breaths, close your eyes and allow yourself to daydream.
- Ask someone to massage your shoulders.
- Change tasks. If you are mentally tired, do something physical. This is especially important for women who work on computer terminals.
- Watch a baby play.
- Share hugs.
- Pet a dog or cat.
- Go for a brisk 15 minute walk.
- Take 5 or 10 minutes to do some slow stretching exercises.
- Put flowers on your desk, in your bedroom, in your bathroom. Plants are wonderful, but fresh flowers are special.
- Keep a thick fragrant hand cream in your desk drawer. Massage it slowly into your hands.
- Have refreshments at an outdoor cafe.
- Go outdoors, find a comfortable place to sit or lie down. Close your eyes and let the sun shine on your face.
- Phone someone who gives you a lift.
- Get away from energy sapping people.
- Sit by a fire with a cup of tea.
- Go to the park, watch the ducks in the pond.
- Buy and send a greeting card to someone special.
- Use fine china or crystal for refreshment breaks
- Look through a family photo album or scrapbook.
- Get involved in your hobby for a little while. If you don't have a hobby, develop one.

Develop a "best thing" philosphy. When you are aggravated, agitated, frustrated, out of sorts and feeling badly, stop dwelling on the source of your frustration and ask yourself, "What's the best thing that happened to me in the last 24 hours?" Now think about that until it crowds the negative stressful thoughts out of your mind.

Nicole Schapiro, nationally known keynote speaker, uses several techniques when she is over stressed: "I surround myself with people who nourish me. I know people to play with, people who stimulate me intellectually, and people with whom I can feel comfortable just being quiet." Nicole, who is also an expert on professional image, said, "Colors affect our moods. When I am under a great deal of pressure I wear a color that reflects my essence and gives me energy."

Get in the habit of using "affirmations." These are positive statements about yourself and your circumstances. Examples of affirmations you might use include:
"I certainly am a happy person."
"I feel enthusiastic and energetic."
"I enjoy being competent at what I do, even though I am not perfect."
"I have the power to improve my life."
"I am a deserving human being."
"I control the excess stress in my life by turning stress into positive energy.
"I am able to say 'no ' to unreasonable requests."
"I am worthy of love and acceptance. People love me for who I am, not what I do for them."
"My days are full of joy."
"I deserve and take time daily to assure my physical and mental health."
"My life is in order, I am content."

This is just a small sampling of affirmations you can adapt to suit your needs. In PART 4 you will find a page on which to make a list of personal affirmations. Memorize them and repeat them to yourself over and over again--out loud when you are alone, and silently when there are others around. You will find affirmations a refreshing stress reducing change. Self talk from the stressed woman usually sounds more like, "I am so stupid," "Why can't I do anything right." "I wish I had some time for myself, but I don't deserve it until I've taken care of the other people who need me." "I'm so disorganized." "If they only knew the *real* me." "I'm so fat."--What other encouraging self talk do you regularly indulge in? When the voice in your head is self critical or depressed, immediately remind yourself of your affirmations.

You will find excellent information on affirmations and visualization, also an effective stress management technique, in Shakti Gawain's book, *CREATIVE VISUALIZATION*.

(Go to PART 4, page 72, and begin to work on your FIRST AID exercises.)

16

PART 2

TIPS FOR STRESSFUL SITUATIONS

IDEAS FOR COPING WITH THE EVERYDAY STRESSORS IN A WORKING WOMAN'S LIFE.

What stresses you? Is it your work situation, inter-personal relationship problems, your physical environment, business travel, personal expectations, trying to juggle a career and family, or just trying to deal with the everyday administrative details of living? In this section you will get specific suggestions for dealing with the problems most common to working women. Of course you will have your own personal stressors, but use these suggestions as a springboard for creatively coping with your individual concerns.

STRESS POTENTIAL EVENTS

A Stress Potential Event is an event that would cause stress if it were to occur. Many of life's stressors are a result of being unprepared. Some stress potential events are major, such as a burglary of your home, or an accident or illness. Some are minor, for example, running out of gas, getting a parking ticket or finding your checking account overdrawn.

Thought, advance planning, and action can minimize or prevent stress potential events. Adequate insurance is a way to minimize the stress inherent in particular situations, for then you alleviate the additional stress of the financial loss that comes along with burglaries, illness, accidents, and so on. Driving on a close to empty gas tank or being careless with your check book invite stress. A quarter tank should be a fill-up signal, and keeping your car well maintained will also guard against inconvenient car troubles.

A serious stress potential event is the loss of security or your job. Have alternative plans of action in mind in case you are laid off. One of my clients, Lisa, was a Vice President of Marketing for a prestigious organization. She had a dream of opening her own public relations firm "sometime in the future." She visualized and planned her career path. She maintained a high profile in the community and was recognized as a competent woman. When Lisa's company was acquired, Lisa was let go during the reorganization. She was not prepared to lose her job at that particular time, but she was prepared by knowing what her next move was going to be.   I talked to her six months after she was let go. She said, "I've started my business two years before I had planned to. But I'm already very busy. The work I did for the company made me visible and now my own business is growing as a result of my previous reputation."

Always be prepared to lose your job. If it doesn't happen you will find that your are serving your employer more effectively. If it does happen, you are ready.

1. Develop a personal career plan. Make it flexible.
2. Develop several marketable skills.
3. Network. Make yourself visible in the community. This markets you, your talents and abilities to people who may know an employer who is looking for someone just like you.

Networking must be done on an ongoing basis. Relationships and trust must be developed before people will recommend you to others. For good information on networking, read Susan RoAne's book, *HOW TO WORK A ROOM*.

These tactics also help you take risks in the job you have. If you have confidence that you are of value to employers and have alternatives, you will find it easier to break out of dead-end jobs. Dead-end or non-challenging jobs are great stressors for women.

(Go to PART 4 and fill out the appropriate section.)

In the past several years, countless women have had the stressful experience of becoming displaced homemakers. (This is the woman who worked to put her husband through college, stood by him while he got going in his profession, scrimped and saved for years early in the marriage, and bore and raised four children. Then when the hard times were over, she was tired, maybe a little overweight, not terribly stimulating, and he was ready for a younger, thinner, more exciting companion.)

My advice to all women is, recognize the possibility of having to take care of yourself and develop the skills to do just that. Do not take the ostrich position. Head-in-the-sand thinking "it only happens to other people" leaves you unaware of the situations that can creep up on you from behind. Remember, YOU are other people's other people. Preparation for "what ifs" is a good stress reducer.

FINANCIAL FIRST AID

BE AWARE OF YOUR FINANCIAL CONDITION. Make yourself a file or get a notebook in which to keep ongoing records. Know exactly what you have in savings, investments, assets, and secure ongoing income. Know where the money is and how to get ahold of it if you need it.

DEVELOP A FINANCIAL PLAN. This should include a plan for securing and building income, long range goals for your financial future, and a system for sensible spending.

BE CONSCIOUS OF YOUR SPENDING HABITS. Do you go to sales often just to see if there is something you might need on sale? Do you spend when you are angry at your mate just to get even? Is shopping a stress first aid technique for you? If it is, this probably causes more stress in the long run. Do not buy on impulse unless you have extra cash and the money is not earmarked for anything else. When you shop, make sure that your purchases can easily be paid for at the end of the month.

KEEP TRACK OF YOUR SPENDING FOR A MONTH OR TWO. This means write down everything you spend. (This absolutely doesn't work if you keep track in your head.) People with financial stress generally spend arbitrarily and wonder why the money runs out at the end of the month, before the checks do.

MAKE OUT A BUDGET AND STICK TO IT. With your financial plan ready, determine how much is necessary to pay your housing, food, insurance, and other essential expenses. Allocate the rest appropriately. Discipline yourself to stick to your budget.

SAVE CONSISTENTLY. The first item on your budget should be your untouchable savings. Read *THE RICHEST MAN IN BABYLON* by George Clasen, a small paperback that can be read in one evening. It's a parable which gives the simplest and soundest advice on building financial security I have ever encountered. Basically Clasen says that every time money comes in, immediately set aside 10% and put it in a form of savings. If you feel this will be too difficult for you, have the money taken out of your paycheck automatically and deposited in a bank, mutual fund account or savings bonds. Pretend that money doesn't exist. You may not use this money except for the most dire emergency. A vacation in the Bahamas is not a dire emergency. Set up a separate savings account for vacations and "things." Now budget and live on the rest.

GET OUT OF DEBT. Debt is a real stressor because it can control you. You must stay in a secure job even if you hate it because you have payments to make. Debt limits your life choices. There are only three things for which you may go into debt.
    1. Your house.
    2. A car that's necessary for work. (Limit this debt. A fully equipped "sexy" car can over extend you.)
    3. Education or things that improve your mind or skills.
All three increase your long term income potential.

MAKE SURE YOU ARE ADEQUATELY INSURED. The essentials are health insurance, homeowner's or renter's insurance and auto insurance. You should have some disability insurance through work but if you are self employed, that's an essential also. A single woman with no dependents doesn't need life insurance unless it is in annuity form, which then becomes a savings plan. A woman whose income is essential to the family does need life insurance.

MAKE A WILL. If you have not **put in writing** what you want done with your money and possessions, (and your children) the state will decide how to allocate what you leave behind. Since you have worked hard and have acquired assets, you have the right to determine what happens to them after you're gone. (I don't mean 87 years old; I'm talking accidents here.)

TIPS FOR MARRIED WOMEN. Hopefully you have married a wonderful man who respects you, is trustworthy, responsible, fair, and wouldn't betray you no matter what! Unfortunately, not everyone is like that. When you marry, you expect to stay together "til death do you part." However, about half of all marriages end in divorce. You should have an agreement with your mate that gives you equal say and control over finances. As a matter of fact, this whole section should be the basis of your financial planning as a couple. If a man says to you, "Don't worry, leave it all to me," he probably means that literally. This is my word to the wise. Act accordingly.

BE TOTALLY RESPONSIBLE FOR YOUR MONEY. Don't trust your money to anyone, especially people who say "trust me." It is wise to ask for advice from various sources. It is not wise to give away control.

BECOME FINANCIALLY KNOWLEDGABLE. All women should have a complete grasp of the basics of money management. Read Judith Briles' book, *THE WOMAN'S GUIDE TO FINANCIAL SAVVY.* Pick up MONEY magazine now and then.

TIPS FOR EVERY WOMAN:

MASTERING THE ADMINISTRATIVE DETAILS OF LIVING

1. Put order into your household. A mess causes stress. There is nothing as discouraging as coming home to confusion when what you need is peace and renewal. It's not necessary to bring order into your life in one fell swoop. You can allow yourself several weeks to complete the project.

2. Clean out your closets and cabinets and get rid of everything you haven't used in the past year. If you have not used it, you don't need it. Organize closets and cabinets in a systematic way and make sure that everyone in the household knows where things are.

3. Stock up on household essentials. There is nothing more stressful than an empty coffee can or no milk for cereal in the morning. Second place goes to running out of cat food and facing an accusing hungry feline. You also need extra stores of toilet paper, bandaids, sanitary supplies, shampoo, and so on. See to it that you have enough of whatever would cause upset if it were missing.

4. Fairly distribute household responsibilities. Constantly cleaning up other people's messes is a source of stress and resentment. Let others know that since you are contributing to the household financially, providing a home, food and clothes, etc., those who benefit from your financial

contribution must take their share of responsibility for maintenance of the household. Learn to be satisfied with a job that is 80% perfect if it relieves you of some chores. Never redo other people's work. It diminishes them and also discourages them from further contributions.

5.   Hire help. If you know that you can't possibly under any circumstances afford regular household help, hire people to do the extra big or especially time consuming jobs. For example, let someone wash the windows, paint the bathroom, clean the upholstery, prepare your income tax returns, wash the car, clean out the garage.

6.   Ask yourself if some of the people who rely on you for transportation couldn't find another means of getting where they are going. Public transportation? Carpool? Bicycle? I found that an inexpensive extra car for the teenagers in the house relieved me of a lot of stress. Fortunately, I didn't have to worry about irresponsible driving. I hope you don't either-- irresponsible driving is a huge stressor.

7.   Organize your wardrobe. Get rid of or alter things that don't fit. If you have clothes that are too small, they will just remind you of the weight you have gained, causing stress; if they are too big, you probably don't want to grow into them. I learned a great deal from a wardrobe consultant. She helped me organize my closets and gave me good tips on clothes buying that have prevented me from making foolish purchases. This was a worthwhile investment.

8.   Stock up on items of clothing that you use every day. Have enough pantyhose, lingerie, and blouses so that you don't find a run in your last pair of hose on a crucial morning.

25

In the evening, it is a good idea to plan the next day's outfit. Keep your clothes in wearable condition at all times. This means they are clean, buttons sewn on, and heels of your shoes in good repair.

9.   Dr. Richard Lazarus at the University of California found that concern about weight, and discontent with physical appearance were very common stressors. Is discontent with your weight or physical appearance a concern of yours? If so, resolve to do something about it; you will feel better. Keep yourself looking cared for by good grooming, maintaining well trimmed hair in a flattering style, and paying attention to the condition of your nails.

10.   Lower your expectations of yourself, and lower your standards of cleanliness. (I know your mother would shudder at this piece of advice--but you are living your life.)   A need for perfection or spotlessness produces massive stress.

TIPS FOR MANAGING STRESS AT WORK

1. PLAN AND SCHEDULE. Two of the top work related stressors are deadlines and too much to do and not enough time in which to do it all. With good planning and scheduling, you should be aware of impending deadlines far enough in advance to avoid the last minute panic. In order to plan you need a planning tool of some sort. This should be a notebook in which you keep your calendar, daily "to do" lists, and other essential information such as frequently called phone numbers, and credit card numbers (in case your purse is stolen--don't carry the planner in your purse). Go to an office supply story and look through the different types of planning tools. Chose one that suits your lifestyle. Planners that are too complex tend not to be used. If you use a computer you can also get planning software. The point is, make sure everything important is written down. Too much to do? Many of the following tips will help you here.

2. GET THE SUPPORT OF YOUR MANAGER. If you have a good manager, she wants to see you succeed. That makes her look good. Often people who supervise your work are not aware of *how much work* you actually have to do. If you feel overloaded, make a list of everything you have to do and how long it takes to complete the tasks. (You should always have this list as part of your planning and scheduling anyway.) Show this list to your supervisor and ask for her input regarding ordering priorities, more effective scheduling, or perhaps getting help. Susan used this technique. She felt she was being given too much additional work, so she prepared a time log for her supervisor. She was quite surprised

when the supervisor agreed that Susan was overloaded with work. The supervisor relieved her of some responsibilities. If you feel overloaded and time pressured, document your work day. Then go to the next step.

3. COMMUNICATE. This is a key to stress reduction. We do communicate with ourselves. For women, this is usually stressful "self-talk" that magnifies doubts. Women also allow conflict with others, questions, ambiguities and problems to work themselves out in their heads. This saps productive energy needed to resolve issues. Clear, direct communication with others defines issues and clears the air. Clear, direct communication with your manager (not hints) will eliminate a great deal of your stress. For help here, read *ASSERTING YOURSELF* by Bowers & Bowers, and *SOFTPOWER,* by Maria Arapakis.

4. WORK COOPERATIVELY WITH OTHERS--BE RESULTS (RATHER THAN EGO) ORIENTED. If you work for an organization you are a member of a team, even though you may feel you work alone. Stress can be reduced if you concentrate on gaining cooperation from others. Instead of wondering if Al will ever get you the figures you need in time to prepare your budget, you can take the initiative in gaining his commitment to complete his part of the project so that you can meet the due date. For your part concentrate on fulfilling your commitments. Recognize that work energy is best directed towards getting results. Stress occurs when egos and personalities get in the way of results.

5. TAKE YOUR BREAKS AND VACATIONS FOR SELF-RENEWAL. Batteries need recharging and they are not even human. If you are the kind of person who skips breaks and

accumulates vacation time because "someone has to make sure that everything gets done," you are in danger of eventual burnout. Short breaks away from your work area during your work day are energizing. You will accomplish more in the long run. Pioneering work was done in the early part of the 1900's by Frederick Taylor, who proved that people who take short breaks get the jobs completed faster than those who plug along without breaks.

I used to be a workaholic. Whenever I took a "vacation" I took some work with me and came back to the office frustrated. I finally learned that if I relaxed completely, I returned to work with new ideas and the energy to implement them. So if it's an official vacation, make it vacation only. Working vacations are really work in a different location.

6. BE AWARE OF PHYSICAL AND MENTAL FATIGUE DURING THE DAY AND IMMEDIATELY PRACTICE RELAXATION AND RENEWAL EXERCISES. When your head begins to pound, your shoulders tense up, or your mind wanders, take 5 minutes to do some deep breathing, muscle relaxation, stretching exercises, or visualization. Fatigue is a sign to go to your list of FIRST AID TIPS.

7. TAKE FREQUENT BREAKS FROM YOUR TERMINAL. Women who spend a lot of time working on computer terminals have very high levels of physical stress and very often the additional stress of high performance pressure. See to it that the light at your work station is comfortable, you have your eyes checked and that your chair is comfortable. The previous tip on exercise is essential for you.

8. STAY AWAY FROM DONUTS AT BREAKS. Sugar influences thinking processes and contributes to irritability. I

believe much of the impatience with others in offices is a result of sugar overdoses in the form of sweet rolls for breakfast, donuts during breaks and candy jars on desks. Heavy lunches also sap vitality, and alcohol at lunch time contributes to reduced productivity in afternoons.

9.   DON'T EXPECT PERFECTION FROM YOURSELF. There is an old cliche that says, "No one is perfect." That is true. People who seem to do everything right are people who have already made many errors and corrected them. You can relieve your stress or performance anxiety by seeing errors as opportunities to learn something.

10.   ROLE AMBIGUITY (WHAT IS MY JOB OR MY POSITION IN THIS ORGANIZATION?)   SHOULD BE CLARIFIED. GET FEEDBACK AND FIND OUT WHERE YOU STAND. Asking questions is a good way to relieve the stress of uncertainty.   If you are not clear about your specific responsibilities, or where you stand in the organization, ask your boss.   Ruth misread signals in her company and was sure she was being phased out of her job. She was in turmoil for several weeks until I suggested she have a talk with her supervisor.   There was no need for alarm, and if there had been, Ruth could have taken constructive steps to deal with the problem rather than waste energy on worry.

11.   DEVELOP A SOCIAL SUPPORT SYSTEM AT WORK. HAVE SOMEONE TO TALK TO.   Women in high level management positions report that one of the stress reduction techniques they use most often is to talk the stressors out with friends in similar positions. **Be careful to stay away from "gripe sessions" or people who encourage negativity. Good social support helps you find solutions to your**

problems. However, limit your unloading and personal conversations to breaks or lunch time.

Join a network or professional women's organization. This will give you the opportunity to get ideas and support from your peers in other organiziations or industries. I know of deep friendships that have come from networks.

12. LEARN TO NEGOTIATE FOR WHAT YOU NEED. You have something of value to your employer, otherwise she would not be willing to pay you. Business involves tradeoffs. You should learn negotiation skills that allow you to trade what you have of value (time, expertise, etc.) for what you need (appropriate salary, benefits, perks, etc.). Read *GETTING TO YES* by Roger Fisher and William Ury.

13. DELEGATE: If you are a manager, your job is to get work done through others. That means you should not *do* everything yourself. Women have a harder time practicing this particular skill than almost any other. Make it a point to be aware of tasks that can be delegated, and learn to delegate well. To learn to delegate read a good book on time management. All of them deal with delegation--an essential time management skill. *THE TIME TRAP* by Alec Mackenzie is one that has stood the test of time.

14. GIVE YOURSELF RECOGNITION. Recognition is a basic need. However, few employers give enough of this motivator. When I have had an employer who did not give me the "pats on the back" I needed, I stopped expecting them from him and began to give them to myself. The woman who waits for her deserved recognition may wait forever.

15.   CHALLENGE YOURSELF. A good percentage of the women I work with list boredom on the job as a serious stressor. It is true that not every job is as challenging as we would like.   It is up to every woman to create personal challenge for herself. You might create a new project to get involved in. Chris was bored with the job she was doing, but saw potential for another profit center in her organization. She brought her ideas to her boss, and two years later found herself head of a division. She created her own niche. If you cannot be creative at work, you can take night classes and upgrade your knowledge and skills, or find some other non-job related activity that will provide a life challenge.

16.   TURN PROBLEMS INTO OPPORTUNITIES FOR SUCCESS. Ask yourself, "How can I take this situation and turn it into something positive? Can I find a creative solution to this problem that will benefit me in the end?" The classic problem into opportunity story comes from 3M. An engineer was given the task of developing a new adhesive.   His attempts "failed." The adhesive stuck but could easily be peeled off. He found another use for his problem adhesive. You are all familiar with his failure. It became little yellow Post-it notes!   Whenever you have a problem at work, ask yourself, "In what way can I turn this situation into an opportunity to learn something, or create a new solution."

17.   PRESERVE YOUR SANITY. Sometimes a particular job is so stressful that your physical and mental health are jeopardized. Evaluate your job. If you have a job that involves unrelenting stress with its attendant physical and emotional symptoms, changing jobs might be the only thing that will help you. A job should give you satisfaction and fulfillment in addition to a paycheck. If you dread Monday

morning, and live for weekends, you must ask yourself what you are getting out of your job besides a paycheck and constant overwhelming aggravation. It is possible to get a paycheck with just minimal aggravation. It's not smart to sacrifice your well being for money. Yes, you do need money to live, but there are more ways to earn money than staying in a job that saps your vitality and impairs your health.

18. ENTREPRENEURS. All of the tips in this section for working women and the next section for managers apply to you. In addition, you have the stress of total responsibility for EVERYTHING. A good suggestion for you is to realistically evaluate your goals and expectations. These should challenge you but not overwhelm you. Entrepreneurs should pay special attention to the self-care tips. Good physical and mental health are priorities when running one's own business.

THE MANAGER'S GUIDE TO REDUCING STRESS IN HER ORGANIZATION

Organizational stress reduces productivity through increased absenteeism, sick leave, tardiness, turnover, errors, wasted time and materials, poor customer service, and low morale. These lead to lower profits, producing more stress --a vicious cycle. Here are some managerial tips for keeping the stress level low in your organization.

Being a manager is stressful. You are responsible for the work of your subordinates and you have to report to your superiors. Most managerial stress comes from having the responsibility but not the authority, resources or support to carry out your assignments. As manager you are often under fire--You need to learn to keep cool. Keeping cool when under fire involves having a variety of responses available to you. It takes time and energy to develop a variety of responses, and because of this I am going to recommend that you develop good managerial skills. Having specific skills will help you deal with your stressors. The first skill you must learn is how to manage yourself. An outstanding book on self-management is *THE 7 HABITS OF HIGHLY EFFECTIVE PEOPLE* by Stephen Covey. Then begin a program of reading books on leadership and management. Go to a bookstore and choose something that is appropriate for your needs.

A question you should ask yourself often is, "If *I* were being managed the way I am managing my staff, how would I feel, and how would I act?" Do serious soul searching. A good manager is first a good example for her people. Here are some specific tips.

1. Be aware of your staff's work load.
2. Give people plenty of advance notice of upcoming deadlines.
3. Do not impose last-minute requests unless it is an emergency and you
    a) acknowledge the inconvenience and pressure, and
    b) express appreciation to the staff for taking on the request.
4. Keep your staff aware of what is going on in the organization, especially in times of uncertainty and change.
5. Let people know where they stand in terms of the quality of their work, in the organization, and with you.
6. See to it that people are adequately trained for their jobs.
7. Back people up when they need it.

8. See to it that assigned work is interesting or challenging to the employee.
9. Meet with your employees to define expectations and roles, areas of responsibility and limits of authority.
10. Reinforce people for doing jobs well.
11. Recognize that personal and job stress intermingle, and that both work and personal lives will be affected simultaneously.
12. Encourage employees to take adequate breaks, maintain healthy habits and take care of themselves physically.
13. Be aware of the signs and symptoms of excess stress and watch for them in your people.
14. Be aware of your own level of stress and practice stress reduction techniques for yourself.
15. Recognize the limits of your responsibility and power. Be human; don't try to be superhuman. Maintain a perspective on your work and life.

TIPS FOR THE WOMAN TRAVELER

By definition, travel, especially business travel, is stressful. In order to be mentally sharp for your business, and remain physically healthy, you should constantly be alert to potential stressors. I travel all over the world lecturing and conducting seminars. My friends and colleagues do the same. We have managed to reduce business travel to an efficient science designed to protect our physical and mental health. The following tips will make your travel less stressful.

- Pack lightly.
- When flying, whenever possible, carry on your luggage. It saves time at both ends of your trip. You know you and your luggage will arrive at the same time and place.

- Get a small foldable luggage cart. Even if you think you can easily carry your luggage, it gets very heavy after a long work day.
- If you travel frequently, join one of the airlines' travel clubs. These are comfortable lounges located in most major airports. Their services include check-in and seat assignment, so you can avoid lines.
- You can use long layovers to get exercise by walking several lengths of concourses in large airports.
- Make friends with a travel agent. Let that person know your requirements and preferences. Once she gets to know your travel habits, she will automatically get what you want. My travel agent knows what seat I like my preference in rental cars, the time of day I like to travel and so on. Now I just give her days and cities and everything is taken care of.
- Have your travel agent get a preassigned seat. Make yourself familiar with the different types of planes so you can request seating where you will feel comfortable.
- Being on time is crucial to me. Therefore I always make sure there is another plane going to my destination city later than the one I am on. If a plane is delayed, if I miss a connection, I still know that another plane will be available. I never have concerns about not making my meeting.
- Do not drink alcoholic beverages on airplanes. The pressure in the cabin affects your fluid retention and alcohol makes it worse. The funny flavored nuts served with the drinks are salty and artificially colored and flavored. You are much better off drinking orange or tomato juice and passing up the nuts.
- Make sure you have confirmed hotel reservations which are guaranteed if you arrive late.

- Don't stay in a hotel room in which you feel uncomfortable. Before I accept a key I ask the clerk what my choices are. There usually are choices. I am the one who decides where I want to be. More than once I have been in a room in which the color scheme jarred my senses or was next to noisy vending machines. I always ask to be moved.

- Check out safety features at the hotel. Locate the exit stairways and determine if you have a balcony or ledge outside your room. Make sure you are assigned a room that is not in an out-of-the-way corner. **Your door should be clearly visible from a distance.**

- When you leave your room at night it's a good idea to leave the T.V. on and a Do Not Disturb sign on the door.

- Open the door only to someone you expect. If the person who knocks says "bellman" and you did not request one, call the front desk to check before answering the door.

- I stay away from cocktail lounges when I travel alone on business. I prefer not to have the stress of unwelcome approaches or dealing with someone who has had too much to drink and has the wrong ideas.

- When I have a choice, I stay at a hotel with exercise facilities. I use these facilities.

- A long hot luxurious bath is a regular routine for me in hotels. Very relaxing after a day of travel or work.

- I like to phone someone in my family or a special friend when I am in unfamiliar places. I get a sense of comfort when I am in lonely hotel rooms.

- I love room service in the morning. A private and leisurely cup of coffee while I plan the rest of my day starts me off feeling relaxed and organized.

- When driving is part of my travel itinerary, and I am not driving my own car, I do not rent small cars. They are too uncomfortable and unsafe.   I like the feeling of comfort and safety when I am in an unfamiliar place.

- When I am driving at night I alert a family member or friend that I am driving, give an approximate arrival time and route.   I tell them to call the Highway Patrol if I am not at my destination an hour after my expected arrival.

- A car phone is an expense but can give you a wonderful sense of security.   You can get emergency help without leaving the safety of a locked car.   It is also convenient for letting your next appointment know you are caught in a traffic jam.

- One of my traveling friends often picks up a bouquet of flowers to make her unfamiliar hotel room seem warmer and more personal.

- I minimize the stress of travel by maintaining an attitude of adventure.   Instead of dwelling on the inconveniences, I emphasize the positive aspects of travel.   I enjoy knowing that I have no cleaning or cooking concerns.   I often pretend that I am on a pleasure trip and treat myself accordingly.

TIPS FOR WORKING MOTHERS

1. GET OVER THE "SUPERMOM" SYNDROME. Superwoman doesn't exist. Even Superman is just a comic book character. Accept the fact that you are human. Your **mind set should emphasize the things you are doing well rather than what you may not be doing.** "Supermoms" are often impatient, angry, resentful, fatigued, and no fun to have in the house. Your home should be a retreat, a place where people feel good and can satisfy their personal and emotional needs. Learn to say "NO" to requests that you know will tax you.

2. PLAN AND SCHEDULE. This time management suggestion is especially important for the working mother because her responsibilities are overwhelming. Research shows that in spite of "helpful husbands," working mothers still take on 80% of the responsibility for household tasks. Plan and schedule weekly activities (shopping, chores, and especially your own personal leisure) on a planning calendar. A written plan and weekly schedule of family activities and responsibilities can help avoid conflict and misunderstanding. However, don't over do it. It isn't necessary to have your life revolve around the social needs of everyone else in the family. Recognize your needs are equal in importance to soccer games, music lessons and little league games. **The schedule must include Mom's renewal time.** Advance planning of holidays, vacations, and special events also makes things run smoother.

3. ORGANIZE YOUR HOUSEHOLD. Mass confusion and stress result when no one in the house can find anything, and

now you, "Supermom," are in charge of the search operations. Each family member (who is old enough to walk and talk) should be responsible for his or her own possessions. It is not your job to find other people's misplaced stuff.

4. DON'T BE A RESCUER. If you always "save" the other members of the family, they will never learn to take responsibility. It's okay to do favors once in a while, but don't let others know they can always rely on you to take care of their loose ends. This was one of my greatest problems. I had a certain amount of "guilt" that my children didn't have a "real mother," a mother who baked cookies for the PTA, drove carpools, and sold hot dogs at the Little League baseball games. I tried to make up for this by taking on some of the children's responsibilities. This proved to be highly stressful and non-productive. It took a long time for me to get over this and it won't be easy for you. "If I don't do it no one else will" should not be part of your vocabulary. If it's not important enough for anyone else to do, why should you waste your time on it? Think about that!

5. GET HELP. No woman can work, care for children, run a household and take care of herself without going crazy! Something must give. Too many women choose to give up caring for themselves. This makes no sense. Some type of household assistance will relieve your burden. If your children are too young and your husband is unwilling to share responsibility, hire someone. You can't afford it? How much will it cost if you collapse? Have you checked out psychiatrists' fees lately? (P.S. If your husband is unwilling to share responsibilities, you have some serious questions to ask yourself.)

6. SPEND SPECIAL TIME WITH YOUR CHILDREN. This is in addition to the spontaneous time you spend with them daily. It doesn't have to be a lot of time, but it should be focused fun time. It should be scheduled on the calendar so they know it's coming and can look forward to it. **The appointment with your children should never be broken.** This will improve your relationship and also give you some relaxation time if you and your children choose activities carefully. If you feel guilty that your children don't get as much mothering as their friends, this special time with them will even relieve some of that guilt.

7. BE A ROLE MODEL FOR YOUR CHILDREN. An editor of a large publishing firm said, "I used to be the perfect mother. When I came home from work, I cooked a full meal for my family, cleaned up, read to my daughter, and put her to bed. I even used to bake cookies and make dresses for her. Playing the perfect mother in addition to being a competent career woman was wearing me out. Finally I realized that I didn't want my daughter to grow up thinking that women could only work if they were perfect mothers first. By deciding to emphasize my career I was presenting my daughter with one type of role model. I knew that she would have plenty of exposure to more traditional women. I feel much less stress."

8. LET THE SMALL STUFF GO. It's not necessary to put your limited time into those things that either don't need to be done or can be done by others. Ask yourself, what would happen if the laundry weren't done today and instead I went for a walk and talk with my son. Tomorrow a happy little boy might go to school with unmatched socks or slightly soiled jeans. Be assured that his chances of getting into Harvard will not be jeopardized by the way he looked in the second

grade. "But my mother-in-law, if she ever saw Jason with unmatched socks and dirty jeans she'd think I wasn't a good mother." If your mother-in-law is going to think you're not a good mother she'll find a reason no matter how often you do the laundry.

9. TEACH OTHERS TO DO HOUSEHOLD TASKS AND RUN APPLIANCES. The short amount of time you put into teaching people to do the laundry, run the dishwasher, vacuum and so on, will pay off in the end. Teach them standards of cleanliness for the household--exactly what it should look like when the task is finish. Make sure to acknowledge people when they have completed a job. The positive reinforcement encourages them to repeat the behavior.

10. LOWER YOUR STANDARDS: More stress is created by the need for perfection than anything else. If drawers and the linen closet door are shut, it doesn't matter if the things aren't folded just right. In spite of T.V. commercials, spots on glasses will not cause you to be ostracized forever.

11. DEVELOP A BASE OF EMOTIONAL SUPPORT. It is such a relief to know that you are not alone! Most of the time, all we want is a little understanding. Unfortunately, most women do not get this from their husbands or "meaningful others." They rarely get it from their children. You need some social support from women friends with whom you are able to share. If you have a great deal in common, you might even share child care responsibilities or leisure time activities.

12. SCHEDULE TIME TO GET AWAY BY YOURSELF ON A REGULAR BASIS. Marilyn came to my Time Management

seminar recently. She commented that this was the first day in two years she had taken time off to do what she wanted. During the seminar, she saw how easy it would be to regularly schedule time off for herself. You should do this also. It is a matter of acknowledging that you deserve self-renewal. After all, you allow that for the rest of your family. Do it for yourself, too. Women who have "private" time feel less stressed.

Use your STRESS FIRST AID TIPS often. Take the time to develop the permanent stress control techniques in Part 3. Acknowledge the value of your personal needs. You are as important as anyone else in your family.

SINGLE MOTHERS: Husband or mate has been mentioned in several of the above tips. That doesn't mean that the tip isn't appropriate for you. You just have to modify the suggestions to work in your household. As a matter of fact, you need self renewal more than most married women because you have the entire burden yourself. So the tips on emotional support and time for yourself are essential. Hopefully, there are support groups in your community (Parents Without Partners is one; perhaps your Y.W.C.A. has resources) with which you can affiliate. The most important thing to remember is; **if you don't take care of yourself, you will not have the energy to take care of anyone else.**

DEALING WITH GUILT

Guilt is a huge stressor for working women. Here are some things to think about to help you get a perspective on guilt. Guilt comes when you are not doing what you think you should be doing, or when you are not doing what someone else thinks you should be doing. **The real question is, who made up the shoulds?** You, your boss, your co-workers, your friends, your husband, your children, your mother, your children's teachers, the church membership committee, the advertisers in the slick magazines?

True, there are some valid shoulds, for example: If you have a job, you should go to work at the right time, and you should earn your salary. You should pay your bills and taxes. You should contribute your share to the running of the household. If you are married, you have taken vows with your husband, and if you are a mother, bearing children does bring with it certain obligations. In other words, you should fulfill your reasonable obligations. Most women are not able to distinguish between reasonable obligations and the unreasonable or unimportant requests that manage to come from those mentioned above.

Are you one of those people who feels that all shoulds are to be treated equally? If you are, you probably feel guilty unless you do everything that anyone else requests. To feel guilty at that point basically means that you feel your life and your needs do not count. The only reason you are alive is to make sure that everyone gets their requests fulfilled. Sound absurd? When I state it this way it does. But many women's behavior suggests that they believe that they really don't count.

I have worked with tens of thousands of women, and a universal complaint is, "I am exhausted after working a full day, and then coming home and taking care of everyone else's needs. I never have time for myself." Women put themselves last in order to avoid guilt. As a matter of fact, too many women push themselves to the point of burnout. They collapse physically or emotionally.

Not long ago I met Lois in one of my seminars. She told me that as a result of devoting her life to everyone else, she finally collapsed and was rushed to the hospital. She woke up in a hospital bed paralyzed. Her body said, "If you won't stop yourself voluntarily, I'll make you stop."

Paralysis was the only thing that could force her off her feet for a period of time without guilt. She was literally bedridden for three months. When I met her, she was just recovering her mobility. The paralysis had been diagnosed as stress. She told me that she was raised to be a "good wife and mother" and didn't realize that she had the right to say "no" to anyone in her family. Until the time of her hospitalization, she was at the beck and call of her husband and three almost grown children. She told me she lived that way because it was her way of avoiding guilt. When Lois was sick and the family had to fend for themselves, they finally recognized the impossibilty of the life their mother was living. Before her illness, Lois and her family thought what she was doing was standard wife/mother behavior.

Unfortunately, Lois didn't completely learn her lesson because she was in my Stress Management seminar to learn how to say "no" without guilt now that she was almost physically strong enough to get back to her old habits. I told her "Lois, you have two basic choices:

"1. You may be guilt free by going back to living your life for others and end up in the hospital paralyzed again. Chances are, if your body stops you once, it will take this form of protest again. By being guilt free because you are doing everything for everybody you will also have the joy of the following emotions: resentment, anger, hostility, deprivation, desperation, self-pity, hopelessness, martyrdom, and a few of your own personal favorites.

"2. You may say "no" to other's unreasonable requests, therefore having time for yourself. This may result in some guilt, but none of the above ugly emotions. (Ugly emotions are those that make you act ugly when you feel them.) In addition, by saying no, you also get out of a lot of unecessary work."

When I make a choice I usually opt for a little guilt. This has a less detrimental effect on my body and my relationships with other people. Somehow, when I take care of myself, and perhaps feel slightly guilty, I tend to be a little more understanding with others, a little kinder. When I give in to others' needs or demands, thus neglecting myself, I often feel anger, resentment and martyrdom. These ugly emotions tend to spill over onto others. In the long run, everyone loses.

This is a quick first aid guide. For more help in overcoming guilt, *THE TYPE E WOMAN* by Harriet Braiker will be helpful. For advanced guilt read *GUILT IS THE TEACHER, LOVE IS THE LESSON* by Joan Borysenko, PhD.

THE FINE ART OF SAYING "NO."

Learn to say "no" to excessive demands from others. When you can say "no" to others' small stuff, even though they might think it's big stuff, you will have time for your big stuff--yourself and your family, or at work, your priorities. This is a stress first aid handbook, not a book on saying no, so I suggest you read one or two to learn that particular skill. Refer to Maria Arapakis, *SOFTPOWER.*

Once you have learned the fine points of "NO," my first aid suggestion is to practice. "I am unable to do laundry tonight, but I do have time to show you how." "I am not going to be responsible for meals every night. Would you prefer to cook twice a week, should we go out, or do you have other suggestions?" "I realize mother will be disappointed if we don't go over there Sunday afternoon, but I need some time to be by myself." And for those of you who are not married, "No, let's not have dinner at my place tonight, let's go out." or, "This activity isn't what I want to spend my money on." or "No, I really don't want to spend the weekend at your sister's place."

At work try, "No, I will not be on the Christmas Party committee." "No, I will not be able to take care of that right now--I need to complete my project first." "Yes, I do mind taking on the extra work." "No, I cannot have it completed by Friday."

Learn to say no to excessive demands from yourself. Not long ago a woman who attended one of my stress seminars said, "I am here because I want to be a superwoman without stress. I want to do it all and have it all and feel good about it." I told her she wasted her money because I wasn't going to try to teach her how to do the impossible.

I told her I could give her many ideas and make suggestions for lowering her level of stress, and that's what the rest of this book is -- suggestions for lowering stress. There is no promise that you will be able to do and have it all. As a matter of fact, I don't even recommend that you try. Trying to do and have it all places excessive demands on yourself. Women over extend themselves by feeling they "should, must or have to" be the most valuable person at the office, get ahead in their careers, be sexy wives, perfect housekeepers, model mothers, devoted daughters and thin. These unrealistic expectations drive too many women crazy, and make the rest of us feel inadequate.

I hereby state unequivocally, it is not possible to do everything. It is even less possible to do everything perfectly. I hope everyone reading this handbook can accept this fact and say, "No I will not make excessive demands on myself. I will order my priorities and put my time and energy into things that really matter, and I know that I count too."

(List your own important "No's" in PART 4.)

PART 3

LONG TERM STRESS CONTROL: ACHIEVING THE LOW-STRESS LIFESTYLE

Extended stress results in the deterioration of physical and mental health. The most immediate and beneficial way to control stress is to take care of the body so it has the strength and energy to withstand the damaging effects of constant physiological adaptation. Shifts in attitudes and expectations also have a considerable effect on stress reduction. Actually, controlling stress comes down to controlling attitudes and behaviors.

GOOD NUTRITION

Several years ago, when I didn't feel very well, I went to my doctor to determine why I had migraine headaches, many minor physical complaints, and why I also suffered from general lethargy and depression. At that time there was little awareness of the concept of stress. My doctor decided to treat my emotional symptoms first and prescribed a drug to improve my frame of mind. Sure enough, I began to feel better.

We have known for years that drugs can affect mental states. Drugs are substances which we put into our bodies to produce biochemical changes. Doesn't it make sense that anything we put into our bodies can affect us? Almost every woman is aware of how alcohol or caffeine makes her feel.

But unless   she is especially sensitive, the average woman does not know how her body is affected by the other things she drinks and eats.

"You are what you eat." An old cliche, but it is so true. There is a direct relationship between what we eat and our sense of well being. The sale of "Tums for the tummy" proves this.   When we eat too much, or the wrong things, our stomachs protest and our whole body reacts.

When people eat the kinds of foods that provide vitamins, minerals and other essential nutrients, bodies work well. When we put things into our bodies that either have no nutritive value or have harmful effects, our bodies do not have the fuel needed to run effectively. You would not think of running an expensive car on inferior fuel. It would not perform well, and would wear out more quickly. Are you trying to run your body on inferior fuel? When the body is not fueled well, it must use reserves of vitamins, minerals and other nutrients just to function. The body does not have the extra energy to cope with stress.

A great deal of research has been done on health, stress and food. There is general agreement that the individual who eats well responds less severely to stress. And it is well known that certain substances do actually cause stress. The woman under chronic stress can make a significant improvement in her sense of well being if she consciously controls what she puts into her body.

Judith Wurtman, Ph.D does a masterful job of documenting the effects of food on one's physical and mental states in her book *MANAGING YOUR MIND AND MOOD THROUGH FOOD.* It's a real eye opener and has made a difference in my diet. A overly simple summary of her main concept is that generally proteins are energizers, increasing mental alertness, and carbohydrates tend to reduce stress and anxiety. I suggest you read the entire book so you will learn how to use food to your advantage.

WHAT TO AVOID

1. ALCOHOL. Most people think alcohol is a relaxer. They sit down after work and have a drink, or they go to "happy hour" at the local lounge to drink with their friends. Actually, alcohol produces reactions in the body that cause additional stress and alcohol depletes the body's store of the "Stress" vitamins, B and C. Sitting down or being with friends is the genuine stress reducer, not the alcohol. Alcohol temporarily makes you forget your stressors, it doesn't make them go away. There is nothing wrong with an occasional drink or wine with dinner. There is something wrong with relying on alcohol to unwind.

2. TOBACCO. Women's death rate from lung cancer has increased threefold in the last ten years. That's drawback #1. Another problem with cigarettes is their interference with the body's ability to absorb and utilize the vitamins and other nutrients in food. The body needs vitamins and minerals to cope with stress. There is also the social stress of smoking. Other people don't like to be around smokers. An eligible bachelor friend told me that he refuses to date women who smoke because he can't stand the odors they carry around with them. The media is full of the harmful effects of smoking so I won't belabor it here. If you continue to smoke, you are a willing participant in the deterioration of your own health and higher levels of real stress.

3. CAFFEINE. Caffeine is a stimulant. It triggers the same physiological responses as stress. Excess caffeine intake has been found to play a significant role in some cases of anxiety and depression. The amount of caffeine in three cups of coffee is about all the body should have to tolerate each day. Caffeine is also present in tea and soft drinks. You should be aware that when you drink soft drinks, you are actually drinking carbonated chemicals. People who are both concerned with health and energetic performance drink water, juices or herbal teas.

4. SUGAR. Refined sugar has been shown to negatively influence behavior and moods. It also contributes to overweight since a small amount has a lot of empty calories. I'm sure you have heard that sugar gives you quick energy. This is true. However, that energy rush lasts a very short time and, because of the influence on insulin production, you will experience the need for another jolt of sugar within a short time. That's how chocoholics are made. One of the worst things you can do when you experience stress on the job is to sit down with a cigarette, a cup of coffee and a donut. You'll be down again in half an hour. Instead, try some of the stress reducers we'll discuss later.

5. SALT. Salt causes water retention. Water retention can affect our moods. It also is a primary cause of high blood pressure. Stress causes high blood pressure too. High blood pressure contributes to heart attacks and strokes. The average American takes in 20 times more salt per day in her diet than is necessary for health.

6. FAT. Stress causes excess accumulation of cholesterol in blood vessels. This causes atherosclerosis and related

heart diseases. Add the cholesterol in saturated and animal fats and you have a problem. Red meat, especially marbled, is high in fat. Processed lunch meats, cheeses and most snack chips are incredibly high in fat and salt. Our favorites, chocolate and ice cream are also loaded with fat. Avoid these. Eating fats also makes you fat. Being overweight is a major source of stress for women.

7. BLEACHED FLOUR. When brown whole wheat is processed and turned into clean white flour, 26 nutrients are discarded in the process. (The part that is removed is the wheat germ which is then sold in health food stores to put vitamins and minerals back in the diet.) However, the flour is then enriched with four synthetic vitamins. The fiber content needed to keep the digestive system functioning is missing. Remember, stress contributes to problems with digestion.

EAT MORE OF THESE HEALTHY FOODS

1. FRESH FRUITS AND VEGETABLES. Fruits and vegetables are natural sources of sugar, fiber, carbohydrates, vitamins and minerals. A raw apple can satisfy the body's craving for sugar and also provides fiber and a host of vitamins. It fills you up, is healthier and satisfies your hunger for a longer period of time than a candy bar. An apple doesn't have any harmful ingredients. Stay away from canned fruits and vegetables; they are full of sugar and salt.

2. WHOLE GRAINS. Grains are a wonderful source of fiber and vitamins and minerals. Cereal and breads made from whole grain flour are also more filling than those made

with refined flour so you get full on fewer calories. This contributes to weight control.

3.   FISH AND CHICKEN.   These are your healthiest sources of animal protein.   They have far less fat and calories than red meat.

SOME MORE SUGGESTIONS FOR
REDUCING STRESS WITH DIET

1.   Do pay close attention to what you are putting in your body, but don't be compulsive.   The non-healthy foods in moderation aren't going to permanently damage you.   It's okay to have a drink or a candy bar or French fries once in a while.

2.   Don't go on a fad or popular weight reduction diet when you are under unusual stress.   You will just get irritable, and may deprive yourself of needed nutrients.   You can lose weight by changing your eating habits to those outlined here.   The personnel manager for a major manufacturing company said, "Since I have changed my eating habits, I find that I am able to eat more and yet I am losing my unwanted pounds."

3.   Stay away from convenience and processed fast foods. They are full of unknown ingredients that contribute to the physiological stress response.

4.   Eat breakfast.   You need to start the day with nourishment.   When you are hungry you are likely to be irritable, and probably tempted to snack on donuts mid-morning.   If you don't eat breakfast you won't have the needed energy to

function effectively in a stressful work environment. Contrary to what you see on T.V., Pop Tarts or Breakfast Bars do not qualify as breakfast. A "danish" doesn't either. Fruit, whole or in juice form, and oatmeal qualify as breakfast, as do other hot or cold whole grain cereals, and breads.

5. Eat lunch. Skipping lunch does nothing for your disposition. If you're hungry and irritable you will be more stressed yourself, and cause it in others also. Skipping lunch doesn't do anything for your figure either. If you skip lunch, you won't have the energy to get through the afternoon and you'll tend to snack on junk or eat too much for dinner. This allows you to go into your stressful negative self-talk routine.

6. When it concerns what you eat, apply this general rule of thumb: If it grows on trees or in the ground, flies or swims, it is probably okay to eat. If it has been manufactured in a stainless steel vat, is a funny color and wrapped in cellophane, you should avoid it. Read labels. If you can't pronounce the ingredients, and if it has a shelf life longer than the 5 year 50,000 mile warranty on your new car, it probably isn't food. Don't eat it.

(Go to PART 4 and work on a good nutrition plan for yourself.)

CONTROLLING STRESS WITH MENTAL RELAXATION

"The best time to relax is when you don't have time to relax."

Learn several physical and mental relaxation exercises to use on a regular basis. These can keep you in a calm frame of mind and improve your perspective on life. I will introduce you to only one of these relaxation exercises. Try it. This technique can relax you in a matter of minutes.

You know that the worry, guilt, and "should" thoughts in your mind can produce stress. As a matter of fact, much of the stress we feel is a result of our own thoughts. If we can think ourselves into stress we can also think ourselves into relaxation. Thinking relaxing thoughts makes our muscles relax. Many women say that their tension headaches go away after 5 to 10 minutes of mental relaxation. Mental relaxation is often called visualization, but it is really what we commonly call daydreaming. When our minds wander to wonderful places and thoughts we feel guilty because we're not concentrating on the issues at hand. But the daydream or mental relaxation gives us a chance to bring body processes back to normal.

Try this exercise: Shut your eyes. Take a deep slow breath. As you breathe in, feel the tension in your body. As you breathe out, imagine this tension flowing down from the top of your head through your shoulders, down your arms and out your fingertips. Take another deep breath and, as you let this breath out, imagine tension flowing down your torso, through your legs and out the tips of your toes. Take several breaths until your body feels completely relaxed. Now let your mind go back to a time and place in which you felt totally relaxed. It might have been a childhood experience, a vacation, time shared with a special person. While you continue your closed-eye deep breathing, relive that experience. Transport yourself to that time and place. See yourself in your imagination doing what you did then, breath that air, smell those smells, see those colors. Mentally live that previous time and place until you feel delicious relaxation wash over you.

Nicole Schapiro, who travels more than 200 days a year, says she often relaxes in busy airports by transporting herself to nature and lush green hills. Another friend replays a fantastic tennis game. I lay by the side of a swimming pool, hear the splash of the swimmers, and feel the warm sun on my body. You choose your special place. Go there whenever you feel tense, anxious, or need to unwind. Practice until you have perfected this technique. You will find yourself far more refreshed and rejuvenated than when you try to relax with a drink.

You can also learn techniques for deep muscle relaxation, meditation, yoga, the Relaxation Response, or self-hypnosis. See the Recommended Reading at the end of this book, or spend time in the self-help or health section of your local bookstore.

EXERCISE AWAY TENSION

Make exercise a regular part of your daily routine. Bodies have joints and muscles because bodies were meant to move. People were not designed to function comfortably in cubicles called rooms or offices, or to get from place to place in rolling cubicles called cars. Yet that is how we live. We are trying to adapt to civilization, and adaptation is a stressor. To get rid of some of our stress, we must use our bodies for the things they were designed to do. People who exercise regularly are healthier and live longer than those who are sedentary. Unfortunately, the working woman is often in a position that keeps her inactive. Most office equipment that women use causes muscle strain that adds to the stressors already present in the working environment.

Ideally, to get into good physical condition a person should exercise actively six times a week. This experience should be aerobic; that is, it should make your heart beat at 70% to 85% of capacity. This should continue for 12 minutes. According to exercise expert Covert Bailey, the elevated heart rate changes metabolism rates and is instrumental in general fitness and in weight control.

Not everyone is striving for top physical fitness. We are looking at stress reduction so other programs might be better for you. Dance classes such as jazzercise have become very popular with working women. These classes are scheduled in the early evening, and for the really dedicated, sometimes at 6 a.m. If you can't quite manage that, there are other things you can do to energize yourself and relieve your minor aches and tensions.

1. WALKING IS EXCELLENT EXERCISE. If you walk at a brisk rate for a half an hour a day, you will be getting an adequate amount of exercise. The time spent walking to the coffee pot does not count. The walking should be done outdoors in comfortable shoes. Robert S. Brown, Sr., Ph.D., M.D. studied over 10,000 people since the mid 70's. He found that half an hour of exercise three times a week dramatically improved mood in 75% of his patients who were suffering mild to moderate depression. Walking is the easiest exercise to do.

2. DO STRETCHING EXERCISES AT YOUR DESK. You will feel better. Neck rolls regularly will relieve neck tension. If other people see you exercising and think you're crazy, that's okay. Part of your stress probably comes from trying to live up to other people's expectations. You can get rid of that stressor at the same time. If you are really shy about exercising in public, duck into the supply closet, or lock yourself in a stall in the bathroom and exercise in private.

3. OWN AND USE A PERSONAL PIECE OF EXERCISE EQUIPMENT. I used to have a mini trampoline in my bedroom. A doctor friend has one in her office. I liked it because it was the ideal lazy person's exerciser. Now I have a stationary bike and a rowing machine. When I am too tired to change my clothes and go to my health club to play tennis or work out in the exercise room, I row while I watch the evening news. Now while I get stressed over world conditions, I can relieve that stress by exercising. When I am not traveling, I begin my mornings by riding the bike while I read. Before breakfast both my mind and my body have been exercised. I have a sense of accomplishment early in the day.

Exercise is so beneficial because it triggers the parasympathetic nervous system which acts to normalize the body processes. When a person exercises, she uses her muscles the way nature intended. This contributes to normal circulation, relieving the body of tension. The best reason for regular exercise is that it makes you feel better.

Sue works out in the exercise room at the athletic club. She grimaces and complains during her whole routine. When I asked her why she does something she doesn't like, she said, "I always feel so good afterward. I have more energy and my disposition improves."

Recent research suggests that exercise also has a biochemical effect on the brain producing clarity of thought and creativity. I know that some of my best thoughts come on the tennis court. Many of my professional friends tell me they have their best ideas in conjunction with exercise. Exercise time is not a luxury for the working woman; it is a necessity.

MANAGE TIME TO MANAGE STRESS

Not having enough time is a major stressor for most people. The working woman with a family has the greatest problem because she must put in her regular work week and also keep up her other job -- that of homemaker. Research shows that the working woman puts in an average of four hours work at home per day after her paying job is over. The man, on the other hand, averages 30 minutes per day in household tasks.

My client, Jennifer, said: "After my work day, I have to shop for the family or pick up the baby from the sitter's house. Then I have to fix dinner. My husband 'helps,' which I appreciate, but I still have the overall responsibility. I seem to be tense and irritable much of the time and have very little energy. My personal life isn't satisfying; things aren't working out too well."

I asked Jennifer what would help reduce her stress and she said, "More hours in the day." Actually, Jennifer doesn't need more hours, she needs to manage the ones she has. Good time management techniques are also stress reduction techniques.

Time management involves making out a written schedule and ordering priorities. It also involves the ability to say "no" to non-essentials and "yes" to those activities that are necessary for your well being. I have already suggested that you read a good time management book, or go to a time management seminar and learn the essential planning skillls. Discipline yourself to use them.   I'll suggest Covey, *THE 7 HABITS OF HIGHLY EFFECTIVE PEOPLE* again.

My tips for this section are first aid tips for scheduling stress reduction time for yourself because too much stress shows up as low productive energy and health breakdowns. Health is a number one priority. Good health is not an accident. It is a result of self care. The working woman must put self care time on her calendar and then keep her appointments with herself. As the administrative details of living call for attention it becomes too easy to "not have time" to exercise, take a long hot bath, take a walk on the beach; but if these things are on the calendar and take top priority, they will get done.

The successful women I work with know that their physical and mental health is a top priority. One of my very successful colleagues told me that she goes to her health club three mornings a week at 6 a.m., works out for 45 minutes, then showers and dresses in a leisurely relaxing way and begins her work day at 8 a.m. One of my clients, a high level executive for a major manufacturing company, said that she uses half her lunch hour to take a vigorous walk. Yet another successful woman said that she schedules in an hour before dinner to completely unwind (without a drink) as a good way to make the transition between work and home.

Every woman can come up with a creative way to schedule self care time. I know that many women feel guilty when they begin taking time for themselves. They feel they are neglecting their families. I do know that those who persist get over the guilt. Their dispositions and energy levels improve, and their families ultimately reap benefits. If you need to, review the section on guilt.

RECOGNIZE YOUR VALUE AS A HUMAN BEING

In a male dominated society, it is very hard for many women to feel truly "equal." Yes, I know we have been given "equality" under the law, but in reality we do not get equal pay or opportunity. The outward struggle for equality in the business world is a stressor, and often our emotional acceptance of our lesser value adds to it.

A bank vice president said to me, "I am the highest ranking woman in this bank. There are three levels above me, and I know I'll never get any higher than I am. The men at my level have reasonable expectations of promotion. My expectations are nil."

When I talked to her, Janet was close to exhaustion. The bank was undergoing reorganization and some positions were unfilled. Work was piling up, and somehow, Janet was the person usually staying late. When I asked her why she overextended herself so much, she said, "There are so many loose ends. Someone has to take care of them!" Janet's behavior, trying to be a troubleshooter and trying to take on the burden of extra minor responsibilities, suggested that she saw little value in herself as a human being, but value only in what she did for others. She was reinforcing her stressors.

She was also inadvertantly limiting her promotablity herself by being a doer. Top management is made up of conceptualizers, motivators and delegators, not doers.

In addition to her work load, Janet had teenage children and spent her weekends on family needs. I asked Janet when she was going to take care of herself and she said, "After I get everything else taken care of. It won't be too much longer." Janet put herself in last place and suffered from it physically.

Her migraines were constant. Since Janet put herself in last place, so did everyone else. When she couldn't cope any longer, she was ready to acknowledge that she deserved help.

I told Janet that she had to see herself as being as important as everyone else. Thus she had to protect her time and her health. To do this she had to negotiate with others for equitable distribution of the work load at the office. For example, instead of automatically taking on extra responsibility, Janet might evaluate what had to be done and then talk to her peers at work saying, "Here is a list of OUR additional projects this week. Let's determine how we can accomplish them. That not only relieves her personal burden but also identifies Janet as a leader.

She also has to express her needs to her family and work out time when she comes first. I found that when I did this, my children were relieved. My "sacrifice" for my children showed up in resentment. I was not terribly pleasant and the children felt guilty for "taking advantage" of me. No one was happy. When I began to say "No" or "Not now" to them, everyone felt better. I was setting limits for them and taking care of my needs. My stress level went down, I felt physically and emotionally better, and this reflected itself in my behavior.

A wonderful book for helping women recognize their value is Ruth Ross' *PROSPERING WOMAN*. I recommend it highly.

KEEP YOUR "I LOVE YOU'S" UP TO DATE

I enjoy reading the advice columns in the newspaper. I get a sense of what bothers people. Many problems Ann Landers or Dear Abby deal with are things that some of us think are ridiculous, but each letter is written by someone stressed enough to need help. Unfortunately, these people don't have the support of friends which is so helpful in reducing stress. Instead, they write to a friendly stranger.

Sometimes people write to give rather than get advice. At regular intervals, someone tells the advice columnist to remind readers to let those you love know you love them. A typical comment: "My father died last week. I always meant to let him know how much I appreciated what he did for me, but I never got around to expressing it; now it is too late." Don't let it be too late for you.

A standard male comment goes something like this: "I work hard to provide a comfortable home for my wife and children. They have a nice car, clothes, piano lessons, the best of everything. They know I love them; I wouldn't knock myself out like this if I didn't!"

Working women are beginning to think and say the same things. Lack of openly expressed love is a major stressor for all family members. TELL people you love that you love them. What you spread around comes back to you.

Sheila Murray Bethel, top woman sales trainer in the country, travels constantly. Sheila and her husband Bill speak to each of their six grown children every week. They use the telephone to keep their "I love you's" up to date. Keeping "I love you's" up to date brings peace of mind, the opposite of stress.

Most people are very good at expressing themselves when something goes wrong, but they have a much harder time expressing positive feelings. This is especially true for people under stress. They have a tendency to find fault or blame others. It does not feel good to be blamed or criticized, and it does not feel good to do the criticizing. Criticism is a stress generator.

Try this technique. It worked for me. Next time you come home exhausted, walk into the house and find several things to criticize -- coats all over the dining room table, chores undone, apple cores, empty pop cans and dirty dishes on the floor of the den and the family glued to the television set -- hold back your inclination to rant and rave. Now stop. Take a few deep breaths. As hard as it may seem at this moment, give your family what you need most right now -- love and appreciation. Let them know that you have missed them and are glad to see them. Find something pleasant to say to them. You will be setting the stage for harmony in the household, which is what YOU need. Then request their cooperation in cleaning up the mess. Ranting and raving may get the chores reluctantly accomplished, but it will also create stressful feelings. You will find that if you make requests in a loving way, people will want to cooperate with you.

I have developed peace of mind in my interpersonal relationships by making sure that all of my encounters end on a positive note.

When you think loving thoughts you will notice your breathing slow down, your muscles relax, and you will be aware of a smile on your face. This is a state of relaxation. When you express your love to others, you will be creating an environment in which everyone's feelings of self worth and love are enhanced.

Don't limit your "I love you's" to family and friends. Take them to work with you. Now I don't mean go around telling the people you work with "I love you." I do mean, show appreciation for what others do for you, compliment them or give them recognition for what they do well. Thank the people who serve you in your business dealings. Working with others in a way that enhances their self esteem will make them want to please you. This will reduce your stress.

Remember to keep your "I love you's" up to date for yourself, too. Go a step further, schedule it on your calendar. This is especially important for single mothers who get little support from others.

I find that pampering myself, because I deserve it, reduces my stress. I love flowers, so often I will buy a bouquet for myself. When I have done an especially good job I reward myself. If I have had a trying day I do something nice to compensate for my difficulties. I also respect my body by giving it nourishing food to eat, exercising it, and allowing it to rest.

In addition to accomplishing tasks, and dealing with the administrative details of living, women must nourish their bodies and souls to become balanced human beings with high self esteem and low levels of stress.

The techniques we have discussed so far can form a foundation for stress reduction. They are various simple "self-care" techniques that are effective because a woman does have control over herself, her thoughts, her attitudes, responses and general behavior. She does not have control over others or over many circumstances.

The emotionally strong, physically healthy person has high self-esteem, confidence, and the ability to make appropriate decisions. She is able to effectively cope with things beyond her control. Turning her attention to maintaining her physical and mental health is the woman's first defense against the destructive effects of excess stress.

Hans Selye, noted stress researcher and expert, says that the person who lives in such a way as "to earn her neighbor's love" is the person who has little negative stress in her life. I like that statement. It's very hard to live that way when there are so many daily pressures on us. I have found, however, that an attitude of gratefulness and goodwill toward others eliminates hostility, resentment, jealousy, anger, depression, and many of the other negative feelings that influence the behavior of a person under stress. Peace of mind comes from being at peace with others and the environment. It comes from keeping your "I love you's" up to date.

The ultimate key to stress management is a balanced life. This comes from work that gives life meaning and challenge (this can be the work of making a pleasant home for your family), leisure to renew yourself through relaxation and joyous play, people you care for and who care for you, to confirm your being, and a sense of gratefulness for who you are and what you have.

PART 4

YOUR ACTION PROGRAM

A lot of ideas have been discussed so far. All of these ideas have come from women who use them to control their excess stress, and all of them work. However, none of them will work unless you do. It is best to have a guide, a program to follow. The exercises in this chapter will assist you in designing a program to fit your needs. You will work out your own action program step by step.

ASSESS YOUR STRESS LEVEL

STRESS TEST FOR WORKING WOMEN

The questions on this test help you evaluate the chronic stressors that are part of being a woman in the work force. Some questions concern your work and others your personal life. Some can be interpreted either or both ways since it is often difficult to separate the effects of work and personal stress. Score yourself on each question: 0 for never true; 1 rarely the case; 2 sometimes; 3 if the statement is true about half the time; 4 is often the case; 5 for a statement that is almost always true.

___ 1. I am not able to make many decisions concerning what I do.

___ 2. I have the major responsibility for my household.

___ 3. I try to please my husband and/or children.

___ 4. I am a single parent.

___ 5. My current life is in conflict with my upbringing.

___ 6. I have no emotional support.

___ 7. It is difficult to coordinate my professional and home life.

___ 8. I have very little time for myself.

___ 9. I feel I do not get paid enough.

___ 10. I am the only woman in this (department, field, level in the company).

___ 11. I have no one to talk to about my job problems.

___ 12. I feel I must perform especially well to prove myself.

___ 13. I feel there is sexual discrimination/harassment where I work.

___ 14. I have very little influence or authority.

___ 15. I have a great deal of responsibility.

___ 16. I operate under real time and performance pressures.

___ 17. Most of my work time is spent at a computer terminal.

___ 18. My work does not challenge me.

___ 19. I feel insecure in my position.

___ 20. I don't get much feedback about my performance.

___ 21. My work is my life.

___ 22. My ambition is thwarted. I feel "stuck."

___ 23. I am aware of my "biological clock" or age.

___ 24. I wonder if I have made the right decisions concerning my life.

___ 25. I feel a great deal of resentment.

_____ TOTAL

This is an indicator, not an exact measure, because some people can tolerate a greater number of stressors than others without feeling ill effects. If your score is below 40, you do not have much chronic stress in your life; 40 to 59, you shouldn't have too much concern. If your score is between 60 and 79, you would do well to practice stress management techniques, and if your score is 80 or over, you should make stress reduction a priority.

LIST THE STRESSORS THAT RATED 4 OR 5:

_____

_____

_____

_____

_____

_____

_____

Do most of your major stressors relate to work, your home and family, or your personal life? This will tell you where to concentrate your stress management efforts.

YOUR ACTION PROGRAM FOR
PART 1: FIRST AID

LIST YOUR FAVORITE QUICK STRESS REDUCING IDEAS. Commit to using them whenever you notice yourself under excess stress.

FIRST AID TIPS THAT HELP ME ARE:

_____

_____

_____

_____

_____

_____

_____

I'D ALSO LIKE TO TRY:

_____

_____

_____

_____

_____

_____

_____

_____

_____

AFFIRMATIONS

WRITE DOWN POSITIVE CONFIRMING STATEMENTS ABOUT YOURSELF, BOTH HOW YOU ARE NOW AND HOW YOU WANT TO BE.

_____

_____

_____

_____

_____

_____

_____

_____

_____

_____

_____

_____

_____

_____

_____

_____

_____

_____

_____

Transfer these affirmations to 3 x 5 cards and carry them in your purse, put them in your desk drawer, the dashboard of your car, or on your mirror. Repeat them to yourself often.

BEST THING PHILOSOPHY AND
AN ATTITUDE OF GRATITUDE

Whenever you dwell on negatives and mentally stress yourself, ask yourself, **"What's the best thing that happened to me today?** There are many things in your life that you can be happy about or be grateful for. List them here. Referring to this list can put your stressors into perspective.

-
-
-
-
-
-
-
-
-
-
-

PART 2: PRACTICAL COPING IDEAS

Begin to use, practice, and perfect those strategies in PART 2 that pertain to you.

STRESS POTENTIAL EVENTS

List your Stress Potential Events. These are situations that would be stressful if they were to occur. For example, illness is a SPE. Then write down what you can you do to minimize the negative effects of these stressors. To minimize illness related stressors, take care of your health, know good health care professionals and have health insurance.

_____

_____

_____

_____

_____

_____

_____

_____

_____

_____

_____

_____

_____

_____

_____

_____

_____

_____

_____

_____

_____

STRESS POTENTIAL EVENT OF JOB LOSS

Always be prepared to lose your job. Have transferable skills, more than one marketable skill, be of value to your employer and network. This page will help you clarify where you stand now, and what you can do to enhance your professional value.

LIST YOUR SKILLS For Example: (*Computer literate, write well, can organize projects, good at persuasion.*)

_____

_____

_____

_____

_____

LIST SKILLS YOU COULD DEVELOP to make you more valuable to your employer and enhance your value to others._____

_____

_____

_____

_____

LIST ORGANIZATIONS that provide visibility in the community and the opportunity to make contacts.

_____

_____

_____

LIST PEOPLE who could be helpful in your career development._____

_____

_____

_____

_____

FINANCIAL FIRST AID

BE AWARE OF YOUR FINANCIAL CONDITION. Make a list of what you have and where it is. Include savings accounts, insurance policies, stocks, CDs, home equity, etc.

_____

_____

_____

_____

_____

_____

_____

LIST WHAT YOU OWE. This includes home mortgage, auto loan, student loan, charge card balances, etc.

_____

_____

_____

_____

_____

_____

_____

THINK ABOUT YOUR SPENDING HABITS. Write down when you over spend, (or under spend) and how you feel.

_____

_____

_____

_____

_____

_____

SET A SAVINGS GOAL FOR YOURSELF   I will save $_____ a month every month by putting money into a savings account before I write any other checks. At the end of the year I will have_____.   In 3 years I will have_____. In 5 years I will have _____. (Don't forget to include interest.) Write down more specifics of your savings plan.

_____

_____

_____

_____

LIST SOME IDEAS FOR INCREASING YOUR INCOME.

_____

_____

_____

_____

_____

_____

_____

WRITE DOWN SOME IDEAS FOR ELIMINATING DEBT.

_____

_____

_____

_____

_____

_____

_____

NOTE: IF YOU SHARE YOUR LIFE WITH SOMEONE WORK ON THESE EXERCISES WITH YOUR MATE.

ADMINISTRATIVE DETAILS OF LIVING

Write down several ideas for coping in each of these categories. *I can deal more effectively with the administrative details of my life in the following ways:*

1. ORGANIZE THE HOUSEHOLD: (A plan for smooth household operation.)

_____
_____
_____
_____
_____
_____
_____
_____
_____
_____
_____
_____
_____
_____
_____
_____
_____
_____
_____
_____

2. CARE OF OTHERS (Children, Husband, Parents, Pets)

_____

_____

_____

_____

_____

_____

_____

_____

_____

3. TRANSPORTATION/TRAVEL: (Ideas for simplifying getting from here to there.)

_____

_____

_____

_____

_____

_____

_____

_____

_____

_____

_____

4. HELPERS: List people, such as cleaning help, gardener, someone for errands, who can assist you with the administrative details of living. Write down the phone number and how that person can help you. (Include your capable children on this list.)

NAME   PHONE   SKILLS

_____

_____

_____

_____

_____

_____

_____

_____

_____

_____

5. SOCIAL SUPPORT: List people to talk to or be with when you need to "unload" or need reassurance or understanding.

_____

_____

_____

_____

_____

_____

_____

_____

_____

6. SELF CARE: List all the ways you can think of to take care of yourself. This might include weight control, a new hairstyle, make-up update, and wardrobe care. (What needs repairing, replacing or discarding?) Use creative thinking in this section.

_____

_____

_____

_____

_____

_____

_____

_____

_____

_____

_____

_____

_____

_____

_____

_____

_____

_____

_____

_____

DEALING WITH GUILT

ON THIS PAGE YOU WILL JOT DOWN THINGS OR PEOPLE
TO WHICH YOU RESPOND WITH GUILT.   THEN   THINK
ABOUT *WHY* YOU FEEL THE GUILT.   ASK YOURSELF
WHO MADE UP YOUR SHOULDS?   ARE THE SHOULDS
VALID GIVEN YOUR NEEDS AND LIFESTYLE?   FOR EACH
GUILTY FEELING, ASK YOURSELF, IS THERE MORE PAIN
IN DOING WHAT OTHERS WANT AND AVOIDING GUILT, OR
NOT DOING WHAT THEY WANT AND FEELING GUILT?
VERY OFTEN, FEELING A LITTLE GUILT IS BETTER THAN
DOING WHAT YOU HAVE TO DO TO AVOID IT.

I FEEL GUILTY WHEN

_____

_____

_____

_____

_____

_____

_____

_____

_____

_____

_____

_____

_____

_____

_____

_____

THE FINE ART OF SAYING "NO"

This is a page you can use to list the people and things to which to say "no." Write down the name of the person, and a statement you can memorize so you will be comfortable when saying "no" in real life .

SAYING "NO" AT WORK

_____

_____

_____

_____

_____

_____

SAYING "NO" AT HOME

_____

_____

_____

_____

_____

_____

MISCELLANEOUS "NO'S"

_____

_____

_____

_____

_____

_____

ACTION IDEAS FOR WORK

Write down things, people, situations, that have been sources of stress in the past. For each item, list ideas for avoiding that stressor in the future or handling the stressor more effectively next time.

STRESSOR   **IN THE FUTURE**

_____

_____

_____

_____

_____

_____

_____

_____

_____

_____

_____

_____

_____

_____

_____

_____

_____

_____

_____

_____

_____

PART 3

ACHIEVE A LOW STRESS LIFESTYLE

Design a permanent stress reduction plan that you will follow for long-term, permanent stress control.

DEVISE A DIET PLAN

I don't mean a weight reducing diet; I mean a stress reducing diet. If you are overweight, you will find that the stress reducing diet will also help you lose weight because it consists of foods that don't contain high calorie sugars and fats.

I WILL CUT DOWN ON THE FOLLOWING:

_____

_____

_____

_____

_____

_____

_____

_____

I WILL EAT MORE OF THE FOLLOWING:

_____

_____

_____

_____

_____

_____

ADDITIONAL IDEAS FOR CONTROLLING STRESS THROUGH GOOD NUTRITIONAL HABITS

_____
_____
_____
_____
_____
_____
_____
_____
_____
_____
_____
_____
_____

COMMIT YOURSELF TO SOME FORM OF EXERCISE

I WILL PRACTICE LONG TERM STRESS CONTROL BY COMMITTING TO THE FOLLOWING EXERCISE PROGRAM:

_____
_____
_____
_____
_____
_____
_____
_____
_____
_____
_____
_____

HERE ARE SOME IDEAS FOR GAINING BETTER CONTROL OF MY TIME

START BY PLANNING TIME TO GET ORGANIZED AND SCHEDULE WORK AND PERSONAL PRIORITIES.

_____
_____
_____
_____
_____
_____
_____
_____
_____
_____
_____
_____
_____
_____
_____
_____
_____
_____
_____
_____
_____
_____
_____
_____
_____
_____

RECOGNIZE YOUR VALUE AS
A HUMAN BEING

HERE LIST YOUR ACHIEVEMENTS, CHARACTER TRAITS AND POSITIVE ATTRIBUTES THAT YOU ARE PROUD OF.

_____
_____
_____
_____
_____
_____
_____
_____
_____

SINCE YOU ARE SUCH A WORTHWHILE HUMAN BEING, WHAT SELF-NEGATING ATTITUDES AND BEHAVIORS MUST YOU ELIMINATE? EXAMPLES: *LETTING PEOPLE TAKE ADVANTAGE OF MY TIME. ALWAYS MANAGING TO BE ON THE "CLEAN UP" COMMITTEE.*

_____
_____
_____
_____
_____
_____
_____
_____
_____
_____
_____

KEEPING YOUR "I LOVE YOU'S"
UP TO DATE

Who do you love? How can you let them know that you love them? Make a list of the people in your life who are important to you. By each name write down what you can do for that person to express your special feelings. Some examples might be to phone your parents more often, or think of special little surprises for your children.

I LOVE   THIS IS HOW I CAN EXPRESS IT

_____

_____

_____

_____

_____

_____

_____

_____

_____

_____

Don't forget your own name here. What can you do for yourself that shows you deserve love?

I CAN DO THE FOLLOWING TO EXPRESS MY SELF-APPRECIATION:

_____

_____

_____

_____

_____

_____

_____

Now that you have worked on what you can do to cope with your stressors, it is time to commit yourself to action.

Fill out the Commitment and Contract and begin to feel better right away.   Then take steps for permanent stress control.

A WORD OF WARNING. DON'T TRY TO DO TOO MUCH AT ONCE, THAT'S PROBABLY HOW YOU GOT STRESSED IN THE FIRST PLACE.   Give yourself credit for each step you take. Celebrate each little victory.

You deserve to live a long, healthy, productive, satisfying life.

COMMITMENT AND CONTRACT

I, _____, want to live a long, healthy, productive, satisfying, low stress life. To do this I must commit myself to a **PLAN FOR POSITIVE ACTION**. I will begin making changes _____ (date) by taking the following action:

_____

_____

_____

_____

_____

_____

I feel confident of success because of the following benefits for

MYSELF: _____

_____

_____

MY FAMILY: _____

_____

_____

MY WORK: _____

_____

_____

_____

SIGNED: _____

DATE: _____

RECOMMENDED READING

STRESS MANAGEMENT

Albrecht, Karl. STRESS AND THE MANAGER. Prentice-Hall, Englewood Cliffs, N.J. 1979.

Benson, Herbert. THE RELAXATION RESPONSE. Avon Publishers, N.Y. 1975

Braiker, Harriet B., Ph.D. THE TYPE E* WOMAN. Dodd, Mead & Co., New York. 1986.

Friedman, Meyer, and Ray H. Rosenman. TYPE A BEHAVIOR AND YOUR HEART. Fawcett Publications, Greenwich, CT. 1974.

Galton, Lawrence. COPING WITH EXECUTIVE STRESS. McGraw-Hill Inc., N.Y. 1983.

Hanson, Peter G. M.D. STRESS FOR SUCCESS. Doubleday, N.Y. 1989.

Pelletier, Kenneth R. MIND AS HEALER, MIND AS SLAYER: A HOLISTIC APPROACH TO PREVENTING STRESS DISORDERS. Delta Publishing Co., N.Y. 1977.

Selye, Hans. STRESS WITHOUT DISTRESS. New American Library, N.Y. 1974.

_____. THE STRESS OF LIFE. McGraw-Hill Book Co., N.Y. 1976.

Witkin-Lanoil, Georgia. THE FEMALE STRESS SYNDROME. Newmarket Press, N.Y. 1984.

TIME MANAGEMENT

Goldfein, Donna. EVERY WOMAN'S GUIDE TO TIME MANAGEMENT. Les Femmes Publishing, Millbrae, CA. 1977.

Lakein, Alan. HOW TO GET CONTROL OF YOUR TIME AND YOUR LIFE. Signet, N.Y. 1973.

Mackenzie, R. Alec. THE TIME TRAP. McGraw-Hill Book Company, New York. 1972.

Rutherford, Robert. ADMINISTRATIVE TIME POWER. Learning Concepts, Austin, TX. 1978.

HEALTH AND NUTRITION

Baily, Covert. FIT OR FAT? Houghton Mifflin Company, Boston, MA. 1977.

Davis, Adelle. LET'S STAY HEALTHY. New American Library, N.Y. 1981.

Hittleman, Richard. YOGA 28 DAY EXERCISE PLAN. Workman Publishing Co., N.Y. 1969.

Reuben, David. EVERYTHING YOU ALWAYS WANTED TO KNOW ABOUT NUTRITION. Avon Publishers, N.Y. 1978.

Ryan, Regina Sara, and John Travis. WELLNESS WORKBOOK. Ten Speed Press, Berkeley, CA. 1981.

Sheehan, George. DR. SHEEHAN ON FITNESS. Simon & Shuster, N.Y. 1982.

Smith, Lendon. DR. LENDON SMITH'S LOW STRESS DIET. McGraw-Hill Book Co., N.Y. 1985.

Wurtman, Judith J., Ph.D. MANAGING YOUR MIND & MOOD THROUGH FOOD. Harper & Row, New York. 1986.

MISCELLANEOUS

Arapakis, Maria. SOFTPOWER! Warner Books, Inc., New York. 1990.

Borysenko, Joan, Ph.D. GUILT IS THE TEACHER, LOVE IS THE LESSON. Warner Books, New York. 1990.

Bower, Sharon Anthony and Gordon H. ASSERTING YOURSELF. Addison-Wesley Publishing Co., Reading, PA. 1976.

Briles, Judith. THE WOMAN'S GUIDE TO FINANCIAL SAVVY. St. Martin's Press, N.Y. 1981.

Clasen, George. RICHEST MAN IN BABYLON. Signet (Penguin Books, Inc.), New York. 1988.

Cole-Whittaker, Terry. HOW TO HAVE MORE IN A HAVE-NOT WORLD. Rawson Associates, N.Y. 1983.

Covey, Stephen R. THE 7 HABITS OF HIGHLY EFFECTIVE PEOPLE. Simon and Schuster, New York. 1989.

Fisher, Roger, and William Ury. GETTING TO YES. Penguin Books, New York. 1983.

Gawain, Shakti. CREATIVE VISUALIZATION. Whatever Publishing, Mill Valley, CA. 1978.

Maltz, Maxwell. PSYCHOCYBERNETICS. Prentice-Hall, Englewood Cliffs, N.J. 1960.

RoAne, Susan. HOW TO WORK A ROOM. Shapolsky Publishers, Inc., New York. 1988.

Ross, Ruth. PROSPERING WOMAN. Whatever Publishing, Mill Valley, CA. 1982.

DR. B.J. EPSTEIN
IS AVAILABLE FOR CONSULTATION, CORPORATE TRAINING, AND AS A SPEAKER AT MEETINGS AND CONFERENCES.
FOR INFORMATION CALL 1 800 347-6828